FAITH F

MW01273284

Seven Easy Steps to a

FaithLift

"An inexhaustible faith for an exhausted world."

David C Rodway

Scripture quotations are taken from the New King James Version. Copyright © 1982 by Thomas Nelson, Inc. Used by permission. All rights reserved

Scripture quotations are taken from the Amplified ® Bible. Copyright © 1954, 1958, 1962, 1964, 1965, 1987 by The Lockman Foundation. Used by permission. (www.Lockman.org).

Author's Disclaimer

Faith cannot be purchased or copied. It comes from a conscious commitment to truth. In this book, my intention is to show you principles of living by faith in God, not methods of faith. A cursory read of the Bible and you will realize that God has many expressions of faith in action. There is no stereotype and no methods for acquiring faith. Instead, there are principles of a vital faith in a living God. This is the vital faith that produces miraculous results. My advice to the reader is to read with an open mind, an open Bible and a heart receptive to God's heart of love. He desires more than anyone that you will experience a FaithLift.

FAITH FILES - Volume One

Seven Easy Steps
to a
FaithLift

*"An inexhaustible faith for
an exhausted world."*

Follow David C Rodway on Facebook and Twitter
Email: faithfilesdcr@gmail.com

Table of Contents

Introduction

My Heritage of Faith

I like to read books on subjects the writer has experienced, proven in practice. Does it work? How? The practice of personal faith in God and its results earned me the right to pen this book series. Here is how to live by faith.

My mother, always a churchgoer from birth, made a decision to accept Jesus as savior in a small Methodist mission in Rockingham, Western Australia at about 30 years of age. At this time I had been diagnosed with what was then known as double mastoids, infections in both inner ears. The pain was horrific. The fevers associated with the pain and the side effects of various drugs and radium treatment further complicated my deteriorating health.

My Dad no longer lived with us. My health put limits on the work opportunities for my mother. There was no readily available welfare assistance. My mother's family were so concerned she told me many years later, they wanted her to put my brother and me into an orphanage.

Our future as a single parent family looked hopeless.

But God!

In the pressure of our personal circumstances, my mother as a newborn believer began to read the Bible in faith. She scrutinised the Scriptures, and on the basis of Psalm 68:5, took God as her defender like a husband and faith miracles became a regular part of our life. Amazing provisions of food, money, even firewood.

My sickness required a warm home – in one midwinter my mother walked to the Woodyard with no money in her wallet and on the way God supplied enough money to give us wood for the rest of the winter. You will read about the details later in the book.

When the doctors expected my health would continue to deteriorate – at that time I was wafer thin and what might be described as extremely "nervy," Mom kept praying and believing God. A prescription of Sulphur drugs had seriously damaged my bronchial tracks, stomach and kidneys and the doctors anticipated infection of the inner ear would someday burst into the cranial cavity causing serious brain damage.

At nine years of age, I was dramatically healed after prayer from visiting Foursquare Evangelist, Jean Darnall. Mother's personal faith in God was vindicated.

My health and mental faculties were speedily renewed. I graduated from two universities as further proof.

Healings, significant God interventions, amazing faith provisions are all central to my life story.
To me, everything in my life must have a purpose, including my Christian faith. If there is no corresponding result or change, our beliefs are not proven and have no place in our daily life.

Your vital faith is power. I have proved faith in God works. I was not born with a 'silver spoon' of the family in my mouth, no huge financial legacy to inherit, but I was born again with an encouraged, proven personal faith in God, as my inheritance from my mother. I have proved personal faith in God works – read on and find out how.

STEP #1

The Power of Your Faith

On one occasion, Jesus spoke from a borrowed fishing boat moored near the shoreline of Lake Galilee. After speaking to the crowd gathered along the water's edge, Jesus Christ said to Peter, the Captain of the boat, "Launch into the deep water and let down your net and catch fish."

Peter replied, "Master, we have worked all night and caught nothing: nevertheless, at your word of encouragement I will let down the net" - Luke 5:1-13. This incident shows how faith birthed in our mind and heart expresses itself. Such a statement as this could be the turning point of our life. It represents a dramatic shift from feeling to faith, from so-called facts to the word of God.

'*Nevertheless*' became a pivot point whereby Peter turned from failure to success, from disappointment to confidence, from defeat to victory, and from a night of fruitless endeavor to a morning of bright accomplishment and results.

All night long, Peter had tried and struggled in his professional understanding to catch fish. He had employed all his learned skill as a fisherman. The careful application of all his extensive experience produced nothing. He had no fish. His boat was empty. He had nothing to show for all his efforts.

Peter could have evaluated what Jesus was saying in the light of his considerable knowledge. How would his business partners respond? He could have imagined the expected reaction of his tired crew who had just finished cleaning and folding their nets. But when anxiety as to what might happen competes with our faith, it becomes an uncontrollable infection of our inner peace and calm.

In no time at all an anxious mind can be a powerful, faith destroying force. Instead, he held his cynical imaginations and fears in check by his, "nevertheless."

Faith has no connections to fear, nor is it a physical feeling or a strong mental attitude. It is an over-riding conviction. But, above all, it is an inward certainty and peace concerning the outcome of a difficulty which we are facing.

It is a faculty of the human spirit. It is something that belongs to the very heart of all of us.

In our story, Peter bypassed the feelings of his crew and broke any personal fear or concerns with his bold choice of faith-filled words. He had suddenly reached into his inner self with a fear-breaking change of heart. Peter's words revealed a sceptical response which showed a very different "reason-defying" change of mind.

The words of Jesus had captured his attention. Peter believed them! He then chose a positive assessment of the guarantee of a catch of fish. He put those thoughts into words, "Nevertheless I will let down the nets." His altered expectation and consequent rearrangement of his ideas shaped his words. Christ's words had directed his attention to the power of his personal faith against the negative realities – the outward circumstances of the moment.

Peter spoke those words out loud. He embraced them mentally, emotionally and physically. His tired, worn-out crew had cleaned and folded their fishing nets for tomorrow. They were ready for breakfast. Now they heard Peter loud and clear above the noise and clamour of the crowd - 2 Corinthians 4:13,16; Colossians 1:25; 2:9-10.

Jesus had said to Peter, "Launch into the deep water, let down your net and catch fish." Peter had replied, "Master, we have worked all night and caught nothing: nevertheless...

Nevertheless, in the face of his failure, in spite of tiredness and disappointment, at the word of Jesus, he was prepared to let down his net which he had just washed for the next day's fishing. He was willing to believe that word, and act upon it in good faith. Peter was passing from the world of feeling and reason to God's world of faith, from human failure to Divine certainty.

Faith often produces feeling, but the feeling is not faith. We can feel faith, but the feeling has nothing to do with the origins of faith. Peter felt mentally and physically exhausted. In the inward man where the words of Jesus had taken root, sprouts of hope appeared which nourished his mind and emotions.

His whole being became refreshed in the process as a new hope seized his heart!

Our capacity to fear proves we have faith. Fear is a perverted faith. It is an overwhelming, controlling force in our life, especially when involving people.

Fear is the natural enemy of personal faith. Fear lives on what we see which raises our alarm and what seems not to be happening. Peter's failed night of fishing had him fearing the loss of the better members of his crew; his partners reduced support and his family's needs.

We can see that Peter had the 'facts' of a night of failure which included a tired body, a disappointed mind with its accompanying emotions, and a dejected spirit! These were facts based on real evidence – an empty boat, empty net, and an empty wallet. Together with the eternal question, now what? The facts indicated there were no fish. His experience and professional knowledge could not change this conclusion. There was no fish to be caught that day.

On the other hand, he now had the word of Jesus; a divine command and promise, "Let down your nets for a catch."

Faith always leaves you with a choice, and Peter had such a choice. In what was he to fix his faith? Peter could do the perfectly natural thing, accept the 'facts' and follow the dictates of professional reasoning, experience, and his feelings built upon everyday common sense. But on the other hand, he could accept the words of Jesus Christ, believe them, and act upon them.

Peter had to make a decision. It was a decision only he could make! The battle was going on in his mind, affecting his will and rearranging the inward self and adjusting his heart belief.

This fight will always go on in our mind and heart when establishing our faith on God's word.

Many of us have experienced the same challenging decision which confronted Peter. That struggle in the heat of fact and faith belief differences can bewilder some of us almost daily. Maybe right now we are facing a faith question. It requires us to make our personal decision as to which path we will take.

Peter discovered his personal faith source is that 'voice' which speaks out of the inward 'self.' It is entirely unworldly. Our heart resonates to the sounds of that voice.

Its origins is that place where the Bible contends Jesus Christ resides from that moment of our being "born again!"

God is within us! Likewise, faith is within us. The answers to our prayers come from a confident vital faith within us. We must first receive the faith answer with an inward conviction before we can receive it as an outward, physical, tangible expression.

Vital faith begins with an inner conviction of the heart. It then influences the mind and emotions and adjusts our belief. Sometimes it is felt - but that is not where faith has its life. Bible faith has its origins within us!

How often have we been told we must face facts?

Facts are stubborn and at times uncontrollable; they say facts are facts. In this respect, they are visible obstacles.

To a certain point, that is all true. But what are the facts? It was once accepted as a "fact" that the earth was flat and that if we sailed too close to the edge, we might drop into space. The earth is not flat, and new evidence has given us the proof.

The world once believed to be a "fact" that the atom was a hard, solid, indivisible thing. Further research and discovery have revealed that to be not the fact. A truth that is accepted as fact today may not be accepted as a fact tomorrow. Facts change according to our knowledge.

We have to be confident that our knowledge on a particular subject is absolute for something to be a concrete fact. And we also have to be certain that there is no more information lurking in some obscure, unknown corner of the universe which would change the fact.

As history reveals knowledge is still increasing, and the so-called facts today will always have to be accepted as likely to undergo adjustments sometime in the future.

Today's facts only represent the total of our knowledge and understanding at any given time.

There are five means of gaining knowledge, and they are through the five human senses of hearing, seeing, smelling, tasting and touching.

These are like five servants who reach out and bring the evidence to our minds. All we can ever know in the natural realm, we must discover using these five human senses.

If we lose any one of them, we deeply miss it in the gathering of knowledge.

However, the five senses have very definite limitations. Sometimes they can be impaired by accident, careless use, the ageing process or be overworked and lose their sensitivity.

They are the parents of all the knowledge we can receive. They decide what a fact is, and what is not! They have definite limits. Human senses can go so far, and no further.

To Peter, standing on the shore of that lake, it was a fact that the fish were not present at that moment. It was a fact that his boat was empty, and nothing was going to change that.

His reasoning powers supplied all the information his senses could give, and when focused they showed him it was useless letting down the nets again and hoping to catch fish.

Maybe that's where you are today, knowing that your life is defeated, that you are bound in addictions which you hate, together with every destructive habit you have accumulated through life. Maybe it is a fact that your body is sick and that your condition is severe with no medical answer. Perhaps it is a fact that your material needs are overwhelming your financial income and you face impossible mountains of debt.

When confronted with a serious and bewildering life moment, with its unknowns we should step a little further into Peter's experience. The next word for us is *nevertheless*. As you know, Peter said this word before declaring, "At your word I will let down the nets."

That word *nevertheless* worked a remarkable change in Peter's experience. Bound by the limited evidence of his senses and its unknowns *nevertheless* broke the mesmerizing charm of impossible. The world of 'not possible' where he acted according to his human reasoning is where he accepted facts as stubborn, undeniable things and accepted defeat.

'Nevertheless' lifted Peter into a new way of living, God's world of infinite possibilities. Peter entered the world with the unlimited boundaries of faith when he heard and accepted the inspired and revealing word of God spoken by Jesus Christ.

This conversation led him to a place where he was prepared to act upon that word of Jesus. He believed it to be more reliable than all the so-called facts his professional opinions had mustered!

The Bible is God's word of 'let down your net' for you and me today. It is God's promise that can only be accepted by faith. Our *'nevertheless'* releases the inward man of the heart. God's promises embedded in our thinking through reading the Bible then give us the foundation for that faith choice.

Now we can override the facts and like Peter enter the world of faith birthed in our heart.

The only thing left to declare is "at your word I will let down the nets." Our *'nevertheless'* opens the way for a God 'shaped' outcome - 1 Corinthians 6:17; John 3:3-7; 2 Corinthians 4:16.

In this context faith is a spiritual "sense." Faith is a sense that is stronger than anything the human life can know! It reaches past the limitations of our five natural senses.

It sweeps past all the so-called facts! It leaves behind it all the evidence gathered by the five senses, and it reaches out and lays hold of the proof of the inspired word of God!

With the word *nevertheless*, Peter turned his back on the evidence presented to him by all of his professional knowledge as a fisherman. He took the hand of faith and stepped out onto the revealing, reassuring words of Jesus: "Let down your nets for a catch!"

Peter turned his back on a night of failure, an exhausted body, a defeated spirit, an empty boat, empty nets and a fatigued crew. He dramatically turned his back on all the discouraging evidence gathered by the five senses. Then he turned his face toward Jesus, heard his word, believed his word and obeyed his word.

With an act of his will, Peter committed himself to the words of Jesus Christ. He then netted a huge, boat sinking quantity of fish.

That is how the word of God takes us past the limitations of current human knowledge. There is nothing we have in this world today that did not spring from the creative word of God. There is life in the Word of God. There is power in the word of God. There is a revealing of the things of God through his Spirit in his word! But you can only receive it by faith. There must be a *nevertheless* in our experience.

These are the facts – *nevertheless*, this is the word of God!

Here's how I feel – *nevertheless this is* the Word of God.

If you decide to choose that Bible truth: If you will look to the promises of God and believe them, you will have an abundant result as experienced by Peter.

God will save you from your sins. He will break the powerful, controlling addictions that bind your life. He will heal your sick body and supply your every need. God will transform your entire life. The power of your personal faith is the inspired word of God.

Right now, lift up your faith in God, embrace his promised abundant blessing, and welcome his working power in your life.

Allow his wonderful healing and providing presence to meet your every need in spirit, mind, and body, setting you free from every need. In the name of Jesus Christ, the Son of God, so be it!

THE REVIEW

Step #1   Know how faith works.

Jesus Christ said to Peter, "Launch into the deep water
and let down your net and catch fish." Peter replied,
"Master, we have worked all night and caught nothing:
nevertheless, at your word of encouragement I will let
down the net" - Luke 5:1-13.

Reflections and personal observations -

My immediate thoughts

My life application

My personal example

My experience

My lessons learned

STEP #2

Faith Insists On Inside Revolution For An Outside Revelation

James, the pastor of the Jerusalem church, said, "It's the prayer of faith that will save the sick, and Jesus Christ will raise them up." Let me illustrate this with Don's life story.

He was a tradesman who worked in our home in Canada some time ago. He saw me holding a booklet I had written called *'God Still Heals Today,'* and he proceeded to tell me about his earlier life. Don had had several addictions which he could not shake off, and eventually, they caused a heart condition and several severe organ breakdowns.

Over some years he tried addiction therapy and spent time in various recovery house programs, but nothing worked. He had heard about Jesus Christ, and then, he met Him.

It was an encounter where he turned over what was left of his life, at 54 years of age, to God.

He discovered that he had a God-shaped void within him; a space for God which needs filling. After making peace with God, it was the prayer of faith that gave him a new start in life which included a complete healing of his physical body.

Ten years later here he was, standing in front of me, active for his age, working his trade, and still rejoicing in his total healing. Don still enjoys the best of health and is taking no medication - James 5:14.

The Bible tells how Jesus Christ met a man who had been seriously ill for 38 years. Described as 'a certain man', he was a typical example of people with serious illnesses who gathered at what was locally called the Pool of Bethesda. Many disabled people, blind, gravely ill, diseased gathered around this pool, most of them tagged as incurable - John 5:1-9.

Jesus saw this 'certain man' and observed that he had been at this location a long time and still had a serious health condition. He asked him this question, "Will you be made whole?"

By this, Jesus meant, "Is it your will to be healed?" That is not the same as "Do you believe I can heal you?" or "Would you like me to heal you?" Jesus challenged the man directly with the question, "Do you will to be made well?"

There was no room for wishing, wondering, and hoping in this question from Christ. This comment from Jesus cut right through to the truth: "Do you want it?"

After 38 years of sickness, this is a very reasonable question to ask. When there is no improvement, believing for better health loses its priority over time. Their acceptance of the illness and accommodation of its presence is easily understood. They now make the best of what little life they can piece together.

Think of one year, or maybe two.... a strength of focused will is of utmost importance to personal faith for a miracle. But, when two years becomes 10 or 20 or 30 or even 38 in the case of this man the human will becomes 'pockmarked' with doubt and uncertain belief.

This man had been trying to obtain healing for 38 long years. The pool where he and other sick people gathered was unique. From time to time, as the Bible described it, the water was troubled by an angelic presence. Healing was immediate, for the first person into the pool following this visit.

There is no mention as to how often this occurred and whether it was during daylight hours or at night.

Regardless of whether this troubling of the water occurred weekly or once a year, this man's 'will' still kept him poolside after 38 years.

This angelic event was impossible to predict. It had not been kind to this man. He had suffered disappointment and frustration, but even so, he was still waiting for an opportunity to get to the pool at the right time.

Undoubtedly this would eat away at his thinking. Why should he remain in this condition? Others are getting well. Over the years fear and despair had no doubt taken root in his thinking.

Now he faced this challenging, penetrating question, "Do you have the will, and want to be healed?" Was this urging coming from just another 'do-gooder?'

All the other health specialists had dashed his hopes. But, this man seemed different. Jesus did not question his condition. He did not offer futile sympathy. He ignored his apparent lack of human help and disregarded his frustration and disappointment.

Jesus Christ asked a question which went directly to his innermost being – the deepest part of his thinking processes – "Do you want to be made healthy?"

Jesus pinpointed this man's barrier to wellness by asking this simple question. Christ encouraged this sick man to release his faith by advising him to refresh his 'will' to become healthy again. It is also our decision. "I will believe and act," is a giant door opener to a productive faith.

Faith for God to heal us is not will-power. But faith does need a definite, deliberate, supporting action of the human will.

Until it is released, faith remains only a potential, inactive, untested force. It is under the test, in the pressure of the circumstance faith is revealed. There are far too many people today who declare that God can do all things, but they cannot believe for God to do just one particular thing, whatever it may be.

Words are not faith; it is the spirit motivating the words which make them faith. Too many people shout that all things are possible, but they shrink from accepting that this one thing is possible. They have no faith for solving the problem which needs addressing right now.

Nothing will ever happen if you have no will to be healed. Fear so often adversely affects the action of the human will at this point. Fear can stand in the way of moving from an inactive to an active faith.

We are concerned that we might look foolish if nothing happens as a result of our confidence in God. We see that our assumed faith may turn out to be no faith under test. If nothing occurs not only will we be hurt by the action but others around us will judge our belief and the quality of our God expectation?

The Bible says that God has not given us a spirit of fear to make us uncertain and hesitant. He has given us energy, strength, love and the soundness of mind, vital to an active faith. Applying this thought to our life can change the entire course of our personal thinking and expression. The inner man stands up when we absorb and accept this truth. It inevitably brings healing and release from the prison of fear.

Personally, I find great comfort and confidence in this Bible truth. I frequently quote it when talking to people who are fighting health and personal problems. "God has not given us a spirit of fear..." - 2 Timothy 1:7.

It is true that we are born with a capacity for fear. But we are not born with fear. A child raised in the right conditions and with sound training can be kept free from the many concerns that restrict and limit our living. Fears also hijack and hold many adults captive in their later years. They, in turn, can pass on their fears to their children.

Psychologists also generally agree that a person is not born with these fears. They come from attitudes formed by living life with its problems, oppositions, and sad circumstances.

As a child, I remember dark nights when local children gathered together and often frightened each other. They would shriek and scream and hide, only to leap on unsuspecting friends in the dark. The faces of especially younger children would often contort with fear.

For me personally, I remember suffering the fear of thunderstorms. Wise parenting taught me to confront these fears. On one occasion my mother took me to an open area and sat me down under cover to watch a thunderstorm. There was lightning flashing, rain falling and the loud crack of thunder seemingly all around me as she sat with me.

She spoke quietly, reassuring me again and again that there was nothing to fear. This reassurance broke the power of that fear of thunderstorms for the rest of my life.

In the same way, the fear of animals, dark, police, water, spiders can be dealt with wisely. We are born with a capacity for fear, but God has not given us the spirit of fear.

True, the Bible speaks of the fear of God as something to be cultivated, but that 'fear' means a reverence and respect. It is not a tormenting, life changing fear.

It comes out of a relationship built upon holding God in high esteem, as a valued friend. Such devotion is not an unhealthy fear but a caution founded on love.

Our love for him over-rides our desires. We do not want to misbehave and disgrace him. This God-honoring, sound thought, and supreme desire is established on our close relationship and Bible truths.

It is also an accepted fact that we naturally possess a sense of self-preservation fear. This fear is a warning to us when danger approaches and when we need to take precautions to protect ourselves.

Some time ago in South Australia, near the City of Whyalla, I was driving down a very narrow country road, barely wide enough for two vehicles to pass.

Coming towards me was a large freight-carrying truck with a load of bales (bundles) of wool to take to the market.

The carrier of this cargo of wool bales had no idea that one of his ties had come loose and there was a heavy bale of wool teetering, unfettered on the driver's side of the vehicle.

It was about to fall. I had nowhere to go because of the thick tree growth on either side of the road.

Aware of the predictable danger, my inability to escape it and the weight of these bales (they often weigh more than a tonne) fear would have me panic and possibly drive off the road into a tree.

Faith kept me unmoved. I stayed on the highway despite the threat. Today I am forever thankful to God. I saw the bale threatening to crush my vehicle, and two or three others fall away from me onto the opposite shoulder of the road.

I passed safely.

THE REVIEW

Step #2 "Do you want it?"

Jesus saw this man and asked him this question; "Is it your will to be healed?" That is not the same as "Do you believe I can heal you?" or "Would you like me to heal you?" This comment from Jesus cut right through to the truth: "Do you want it?"

Reflections and personal observations -

My immediate thoughts

My life application

My personal example

My experience

My lessons learned

STEP #3

Living Faith and Dead Faith

People who practice their faith in God have amazing, unexplainable experiences. They freely acknowledge them to be the result of their personal faith. Their view seems to equip them with the second kind of sight.

They see more than just the difficult circumstances. God appears to be right beside them. He walks with them through every storm in life and acts as the problem breaker at all times. Can they prove it? No, but their life is the proof. They so often end up with stories they attribute to God working in their life in unique ways which are far from normal. Answers to life events which are not natural.

Nothing else touches the Father's heart as much as when we trust him. We leave behind our ideas no matter how rational they appear and believe Him. Then God creates a way using amazingly different solutions to whatever the problem.

All of us remember that Israel marched seven times around the walls of Jericho. That was God's strategy for ultimate victory. Israel did as God asked – that's trust - and without any fighting, those walls collapsed. That's not natural - Hebrews 11:6; Proverbs 3:5-6.

As James Dobson said, "Trust is letting go, knowing God will catch you!" How can you be sure that he will save you? It all comes back to expectant faith.

We have met people who at one time would pray over anything and everything! If they misplaced their reading classes, they would pray and find them immediately. But sadly this kind of belief is becoming less and less among believers today.

Is that because we have become sceptical of faith? Or, do we consider the increase of human knowledge to have replaced the super-natural today?

Does God no longer require the five loaves and two fishes?

Does he not need a faith that throws the net on the other side of the boat after fishing all night and catching nothing? We can so easily lose our faith expression!

Jesus Christ identified the source of this loss when he said, "the enemy comes to steal, kill and destroy." His primary aim is to take our faith in the living God and leave us with the dead shell of a lifeless religion - John 10:10; 16:13.

To receive things from God, we must first believe the Bible truth, his word of promise! He does not shower his choice blessings upon anyone in an unbelieving world.

God has established the law of prayer and faith. They are mutually dependent upon each other for anything that is achieved spiritually in this physical world.

Prayer never obtained anything from God unless faith is present. Similarly, faith never receives anything from God, unless prayer makes a certain request.

Prayer and faith work harmoniously together. Both are necessary for their distinct functions but are entirely different by nature.

Prayer is the voice of the soul, while faith is the language of the spirit. It is only through prayer that the soul of man can establish communion with the Creator, and it is only through faith that success comes.

Over time, our prayer can become less emphatic, and our conviction about answers can fall off as an expectation. We are less interested in having faith in God's Bible truths for answers in our life.

Prayer is often quickly forgotten as a force for a change, becoming a predictable ritual. Prayer has a place as a good luck charm, occasionally used when significant issues arise.

Some believers act as if God cannot do very much in this life. This attitude sets limits on what they prayerfully believe God will do each day. It divides Bible promises into two categories.

A small group of promises which we can expect today here on earth, and a far larger number of remaining promises which will be ours when we get to live in heaven. These believers still give a standard confession of faith like, "I have faith in God who answers prayer." But, the vibrant trust and belief that God will deliver us from this storm are missing. And so are answers to prayer!

Rarely is it said, "Let's go after this problem in the name of the Lord right now." It seems some have mentally pushed most Bible promises into the distant future which never arrives in their lifetime. They are faithful believers without an operating personal faith.

Prayer is not an easy, intellectually satisfying practice for most people.

Our prayer may falter, and sometimes we may be ready to give up. Faith then gets behind its twin brother and gives it a boost over the top. When prayer weakens, faith will wrestle with the truth and fight on with a grim determination.

Remember Jacob's all-night wrestle with the Angel? Jacob said, "I will not let you go except you bless me." That's faith in action!

Man's insufficiency and God's lavish sufficiency creates the foundation for powerful prayer. Prayer contrasts man's need with God's willingness to supply it. Faith is persistent, forceful and demanding in its nature. Faith never returns empty-handed after seeking God.

Faith is amply rewarded for its persistence, but it is God who is the giver of all good things!

When faith ceases to pray, it ceases to live!

Prayer requires us to believe what we cannot prove.

Faith does the impossible because it invites God to undertake for us and with God nothing is impossible.

It is only God who can move mountains, whatever those enormous obstacles might be.

It is a faith-filled prayer that moves God!

Prayer that creates great faith solutions centres itself on Jesus Christ and has a firm conviction that what the Bible promises is the answer - Matthew 21:21-22; Mark 11:24.

We all want to have a steadily growing relationship with God, built upon effective, personal faith. Here's how!

Faith grows by meditating on the Word of God. Faith comes by hearing the Word of God, and that means hearing and digesting what the Word of God has to say about the particular matter we are facing. Hearing the Word of God proclaimed is fundamental to building solid faith foundations - Romans 10:17.

So we read the Word of God with our ears open and our heart tuned into what God is saying. Studying the Bible together with others who are like-minded will also help us increase faith. We must never forget our need for newfound faith for every challenge that comes our way in life.

Each faith opportunity we confront in our life will require a different response.

Here are four Bible examples:
- five loaves and two fishes to feed thousands
- five smooth stones and a slingshot for that giant Goliath
- throw the fishing net on the other side of the boat for a big catch
- wash your eyes in that specifically named pool of water and you will see!

These diverse, faith-motivated actions promote an ever-widening expression of faith and our need to listen to God in our personal life journey.

Next, we should realize that faith grows as we walk God's Spirit-directed way. Faith is a fruit of the Spirit, and it needs to have a growing expression in our life along with love, joy, peace, long-suffering and the other portions of this fruit. As we live in the Spirit and walk day by day in the Spirit, faith grows stronger and stronger.

To live in the Spirit means to live in the knowledge and assurance of our dynamic new life in Christ. With this comes a growing awareness that Jesus Christ dwells in us in all his fullness - Galatians 5:22; Colossians 2:9-10.

As we exercise our body to keep it fit so, we must happily and willingly use our relationship with God through his word, those Bible truths. By doing this, we can have a healthy walk in the Spirit and an ever-growing faith.

Our praise is directed towards God, speaking highly of his nature, character, and creative power. These ingredients for praise ranks it as the highest form of prayer. Our praise of God always strengthens our faith as it underlines our relationship through our speaking well of the living God and all that he has done in our lives.

It follows that faith develops by exercise. Faith, like any natural muscle, grows with a widening variety of applications in our daily living.

James in the Bible book named after him states that faith without works is dead. Put bluntly, faith that doesn't work is dead.

Living faith works! As you make your faith productive, it strengthens and develops, becoming increasingly efficient.

Matthew Arnold, a great writer of the past, wrote, *"Use your gifts wisely, and they shall be enlarged."*

It was Jesus Christ in his parable of the talents who showed that if you fully use your skills, then God will double them and then double them again.

Throughout life our talents will be strengthened, broadened and multiplied particularly those grown by faith - James 2:14-26; Matthew 25.

Faith thrives on prayerful activity. If you would strengthen your faith, you must use it, and exercise it regularly! If you fail, don't fret about it, just keep on making your faith work by keeping your confidence in God's Word.

All the while allowing the Holy Spirit to make real what he wants you to do in the process of faith expression. Remember, we do the possible, and then God takes over and does the impossible, but it starts with our simple expression of faith.

A child learning to walk has many falls, but as confidence grows the child tumbles less and less. There are no rules for learning to walk. All children show you that it is just practice and persistence. For a moment, pause and think about what we do as parents. We encourage! We earnestly coach our child so making the learning easier, and piece by piece removing all doubt that they too will walk.

The practice of faith in little matters is as important as exercising faith on important occasions. Remember, David the shepherd boy dealt with the bear and the lion first while shepherding the sheep.

Overcoming adversities prepares us for dealing with our Goliath who in this expression was threatening the nation, Israel.

Every expression of faith builds layer upon layer of expectation for faith success.
We develop a personal library of faith stories which will encourage us in day-by-day living.

These experiences of God at work, when retold, will always break the power of despondency that arises in the life of others!

Be aware that real faith recognizes the facts.
The facts showed Goliath as a giant of a man, a thoroughly tested warrior, and Israel was a scared and anxious military force. You cannot avoid the facts. But David's personal faith was bigger than those obstacles.

Faith says, "God is more than able." Faith turns to God, and we raise our expectation to where our faith rises above these facts.

We know, that we know, that we know this belief in God's ability streams out from within us.

It comes from our heart, the very center of the inner man of our vibrant life-filled being. Nothing will hurt me! Faith then selects five smooth stones - Luke 10:19; Mark 10: 27.

THE REVIEW

Step #3   Believe the Bible.

To receive from God, we must first accept that God has established the law of prayer and faith. Prayer never obtained anything from God unless faith was present. Faith never received anything from God unless prayer made a request.

Reflections and personal observations -

My immediate thoughts

My life application

My personal example

My experience

My lessons learned

STEP #4

Faith in Action

It was a bitterly cold winter's day. The strong, gusting, rain-filled westerly winds from the Indian Ocean had lashed our small, rented apartment all day.

As a skinny six-year-old, I was recovering from a serious illness, so keeping the home warm was essential. A wood fire was the only heating we had, and now the last piece of timber was being placed on the fire.

"We must get some more wood," my mother declared. She then dressed me in my warmest clothing, saying, "I am going to the wood store, and you must come with me as the walk will keep you warm."

It was mid-afternoon when we left our home on Walcott Street, passed the Forrest Park Methodist Church, and then briskly walked alongside the Forrest Park.

Suddenly a very strong wind blew across the extensive parkland. Leaves, twigs, and loose ground material rained down upon us. Almost from nowhere a piece of paper fastened itself to my mother's leg.

She bent down and grasped the paper quickly, looked carefully at it, she exclaimed, "Thank you, Jesus!" It was a Ten Pound banknote (Australian currency at the time). She put the money in her empty purse. We continued walking on to the wood store at the end of the park, where the owner was securing the last load for the day. He had just enough room in his truck for our Ten Pound stack which proved to be enough wood for the rest of winter!

When we arrived home, the wood had already been delivered and very soon we had a cheery, crackling log fire. Our home was warm and cosy again. Over the evening meal, we gave thanks to our good God.

My mother taught me a lot about faith.

She lived it!

She acted in agreement with her faith and walked to the wood store before having enough money for the purchase.

Faith is always what we have before the event!

My mother had that unique show of determination. It was not that she was stubborn, although it could appear to be that. Rather, she demonstrated a resolute, single-minded, 'God can' attitude.

Personal faith grows by our 'feeding' on and applying God's written truth. The Bible is a vast reservoir of God's promises which provide safe, secure answers for daily life events. As a result, we become more and more open to 'unusual' solutions.

The Word of God inspired by the Holy Spirit then flows out of us as a faith conviction and has us walking to the wood store with no money.

These thoughts baffle our mind and emotions as we release them like Peter with our *'Nevertheless, at your word I will let down my net of faith.'*

This faith as demonstrated by the need for something as basic as wood to burn is persistent, forceful and demanding. This personal faith never returns empty-handed after seeking God, the giver of all good things. It is always amply rewarded for its persistence - Romans 12:3; Matthew 21:21. We must communicate our faith for it to become fertile, activated.

Experience shows every Kingdom has a protocol or accepted method for communicating with its Monarch. God's Kingdom is no exception. The method of contact with God is prayer.

Faith is essential to effective prayer because ultimately prayer is simply faith through spoken words taking possession of God's unlimited inheritance.

Prayer and faith only keep alive through their dependency on one another. Separated they each wither and dry up.

Prayer and faith always connect man's need and God's willingness to supply.

Prayer puts into words our believing faith resident in our heart.

God always wants our prayer communication to have the conviction of faith behind it.

When faith ceases to pray, it ceases to live.

Only God can move impossible situations, but faith-filled prayer moves God!

The faith which creates powerful praying is a faith that centres itself on Jesus Christ.

He stated several times, whatever Bible promise you ask God for in my Name he will bring it to pass – John 15:16; 16:23; Matthew 21:21; Ephesians 3:20.

The 19th-century Christian statesman D. L. Moody stated, "I suppose that if all the time I have prayed for faith were put together, it would amount to many months, even years. I used to say, "What we want is faith. If we only had faith, we could turn Chicago upside down or rather, right side up! I thought that some day faith would come down and strike me like a lightning bolt. But faith did not seem to come!"

DL Moody goes on to say. "One day I read in Romans 10:17, 'Now faith comes by hearing and hearing by the word of God.'

I closed my Bible and prayed for faith. I opened my Bible and began to study, and faith has been growing in my life ever since."

The key to faith is the Word of God. What does the Bible say about the matter?

If every answer came from God without hesitation, we would never really know the strength of faith. In the delay, we have opportunities to sort out the unwanted baggage in our personal life which hinders faith.

Problems, circumstances and even storms surround us.

When handled by faith in the course of the overall expectation; they deepen the roots of our character in God's Word.

Be confident of this important statement - delay is not a denial of our faith request.

It is in fact, the shaping of our nature in God and it continues throughout our journey.

Every storm requires our actions – boarding up the windows, securing loose items. So there may be moments of exposure to the adversity, but we get through it comfortably with not much more than 'wet feet.'

What produces this safe landing? Bible-based faith prepared in lock step with an active prayer life will get us through every storm of life. Each time we will emerge stronger and wiser because of those challenges.

In his response to the news that his friend Lazarus was very sick, Jesus demonstrated how to handle a storm. Mary and Martha asked him to come as he was just a few days travel away from their home at the time - John 11:1-46.

Think about the immediate response of Jesus to this request. It was a positive confession of faith.

He declared that this sickness would not be fatal and that both God and His Son would come away with the glory which comes with a miracle. This strong declaration of faith was but the beginning of a long hazardous journey of faith in which Jesus features.

At the end of that faith journey we find him standing at the tomb of Lazarus, still strong, confident and utterly unwavering in his faith and saying, "Did I not tell you that if you believed, you would see the glory of God?"

Between this great confession of faith, when receiving the news of the sickness of his friend Lazarus and his final appeal for others to join him in believing for resurrection, there were lots of obstacles. Many of those barriers were people with fatal 'infections' in their faith.

It was only four days in time and a few miles in travel distance. But, as a venture in faith, it was a journey full of pitfalls, false perceptions and unhealthy talk.

Challenges initiated by unbelief, fear, confusion, and scepticism among the people in the crowd who were around him.

We also may have to contend with these obstacles in our journey of faith. Faith often includes a time of waiting between our asking in prayer for a miracle and when it happens.

In this waiting time, our mind must remain poised and ready for positive results as wrong attitudes, crippling doubt-filled thinking and misunderstandings about faith surface.

As we commit to reading the Bible, especially the Gospels, allow His word to work changes in us with a *"Nevertheless,* at your word we will let down the net" conclusion.

When Jesus said, "Let us go to Judea," it was said with the intention of raising Lazarus from death. He was going to perform a miracle for the glory of God. But when his disciples heard him say that, all they could think of was persecution, stoning, death, and disaster.

"Master," they said, "The Jews want to stone you to death, and you are going there again?"

The mention of Judea raised not only the possibility of seeing conflict but now fear filled their vision.

Fear misinterprets every sign.

Fear misunderstands all we see or hear. Fear puts a negative spin on the circumstances, dilutes our faith attention and, if allowed, changes the purpose of the journey.

Jesus said Judea because he was going there for a miracle! He now had to break through the barrier of fear in the minds of his disciples and the others that he met on the way.

We too must break through the wall of fear if we would commence the faith journey which culminates in a miracle, a supernatural result.

Jesus then quietly explained to his disciples that Lazarus had died. He used the word 'sleep.' The disciples replied, "Lord if he sleeps he will recover." Then Jesus said plainly, "Lazarus is dead."

It's ridiculous to think that Jesus would take this journey with all its obstacles merely to awaken Lazarus from a siesta! How confused the disciples were about the real situation!

They harbored fear, anxiety and worried about what might happen to their Master (and to themselves) and this mixture of emotions totally confused them.

They could not grasp the facts. They were hazy about the kind of miracle that was needed.

How could they have faith in these circumstances? And how can we have a miracle-working faith if we are confused about the miracle we need?

For example, if we've never seen Christ as our need for establishing peace with the living God we will never experience the miracle of the new birth.

John, the disciple who had a very close association with Jesus made this statement in one of his books: 'for this purpose the Son of God came that he might destroy the works of the devil.'

Jesus came to heal all those oppressed by the devil, the Bible says. Sickness is the devil's expression, and Christ came to break its power. Let us all be clear about the miracle that we need! We need to have complete faith in the Father God and unshakable authority over the devil's power in our faith expectation.

Jesus Christ has given us that authority. He has given us his name to use because the devil has never forgotten that he was defeated once and for all by Jesus Christ. Use the name of Jesus with the authority that goes with it. Jesus has defeated Satan and his evil hosts and has delegated to every believer the authority over all things – 1 John 3:8; Acts 10:38.

In Luke 10:19, Jesus said, "Behold I give you power." This verse is your authority to tread on serpents and scorpions, the symbols of the evil powers, and you have authority over all the power, force, strength and ability of the enemy, and nothing shall damage or hurt you.

Turn your eyes to Father God and speak to him in the quiet, confident voice of perfect faith. He will hear you. Ask according to his Word and according to his promise. And he will always hear you! Now turn to the enemy. Face the open cave of sin, darkness, and death with a firm voice of authority. Command! The enemy must give way to your faith-filled authority.

The Bible says, "Resist the devil, and he will run from you." Lazarus came out of the tomb. He was struggling and hobbling along bound hand and foot dressed in burial cloths, which had been wound around him. But, he was alive!

They set him loose and let him go. It was a miracle of triumphant faith – James 4:6-7. And our Lazarus will come out of the grave of dark despair and defeat.

From the cave of death, our miracle will emerge as evidence of the Glory of God! As Jesus said, "Didn't, I say to you that if you would believe you would see the Glory of God?"

THE REVIEW

Step #4 State your faith.

We must communicate our faith for it to become fertile, and activated. Prayer and faith always connect Man's need and God's willingness to supply. Prayer puts into words the intent of the believing faith that resides in our heart.

Reflections and personal observations -

My immediate thoughts

My life application

My personal example

My experience

My lessons learned

STEP #5

Release from Personal Faith-Destroying Guilt

Very few people dispute the moral teaching of Jesus Christ. It has been a beacon of light to every generation since his death.

Here is a record of a crowd response to his message: "The people were astonished at his teaching, for he taught them as someone who knew what he was talking about, having authority, and not as the religious teachers of the day."

Jesus spoke with conviction the truth he believed. His delivery left the hearer with no doubt as to that belief. His passion and conviction compelled the listener to respond.

His authority reflected in the words he spoke demanded the hearer's attention and action.

He taught the people and also demonstrated his teaching.

He dealt with 'thorny' social matters of the day, healed the sick, restored the mentally and emotionally disturbed and gave advice to the religious establishment of his time - Matthew 7:28-29.

On many occasions, Jesus Christ illustrated that before personal faith could operate the individual must accept healing from the controlling power of personal guilt.

An example! The scribes, lawyers and Pharisees who opposed Christ came to him, forcing a woman whom they had caught in an adulterous act to go with them - John 8:1-11.

This group of Jewish leaders very publicly announced the nature of the sin of this woman as they 'bullied' their way through a crowd! It was early in the day, and the crowd was already gathering in the place where Jesus sat speaking. Jesus was always worth hearing.

The Master addressed the crowd from a seated position which indicated his recognized position of authority as a teacher. The people had heard him in their synagogues, villages, and open fields and were now delighted to hear him speak in the precincts of the prestigious worship center of Jerusalem, the Temple.

These senior leaders interrupted Jesus Christ.

They stood in front of him with this accused woman. Their self-importance was displayed. They were so preoccupied with, in their eyes, her proven guilt; they already had her condemned, judged and sentenced to being stoned to death outside the city gates. She was an unclean law-breaker whom they had caught in the very act.

It would seem that in their haste to expose Jesus as a weak teacher who protected lawbreakers, they too broke the law. Under the Law of Moses, she was unclean and not allowed into the sanctified temple. In trying to destroy Christ's reputation they had ruined their own.

The Pharisees knew that Jesus had compassion for the weak and the sinful! If he were to say, "Let her go," he would be breaking the law of the Jews. For him to say, "stone her" he would be breaking the civil law of the Roman government, and this would be inconsistent with his teaching on forgiveness and mercy.

These hard-hearted, relentless accusers had an ulterior motive in accusing the woman publicly. They wanted to trap Jesus and show their world that he was a false teacher.

The Pharisees worked hard at finding sinners in their sin, but were themselves, sinners, as Jesus explained earlier when speaking of them: "for they say, and do not..."

They were known to be severe in judging the sin of others, but able to justify their sin.

Paul in writing to the Christians in Rome taught strongly on this, no doubt drawing from his past religious lifestyle and many associations with Jewish teachers - Matthew 23:27; Romans 2 and 3.

In the meantime, can you imagine the panic among the disciples of Jesus when the Pharisees paraded the guilty woman before them? They were friends of the teacher, and his movement had gained some traction, especially since the feeding of the 5,000 men and then the 4,000 men along with the many miracles including raising the dead!

Among themselves, the disciples would be saying, "We cannot win. Surely the Master will forgive her and let her go, and then what? The law is clear on what she's done." - Leviticus 20:10; Deuteronomy 22:20-24.

The accusers could also 'smell' victory. They never doubted the correctness of their action and had no thought of defecting to a new way of living as taught by Jesus Christ. Jesus had made his purpose abundantly clear; "I have not come to call the righteous, but the sinners to repentance.

The Son of Man has come to seek and to save those who are lost." He inferred these men were very hard of hearing and resisted his teaching on what God finds unacceptable.

These religious leaders were happy with their interpretation of the law of Moses. They thought it was their job to be God's police force. They were satisfied with their insights into the law, and they kept trying to make their ideas work!

In the meantime, they opposed everything Jesus said, even though the evidence was mounting against their accusations. For Jesus continued to heal the sick, raise the dead and set men and women free from demonic powers.

Is not adultery one of the bigger sins as it destroys the foundation of the marriage relationship? Christ's accusers sense they are in control.

The law is the law, and when broken the established penalty is the penalty. Any lesser punishment is unthinkable. Jesus had taught adultery is a sin but no more so than gossip, slander, murder, and lies. To him, sin is any action which contravenes Bible truth. Any action that does not meet the approval of, "Love the Lord your God with all your heart and love your neighbor as yourself" is a sin.

What is Jesus to say to this woman? What is Jesus to say to these men who caught her in this sin that morning? - Matthew 22:37-39.

Jesus speaks first! "He who is without sin among you and me, let him be the first one to throw the stone."

The Law of Moses required the witness to the incident to throw the first stone. What they had made a legal issue had suddenly become a moral issue. These self-righteous men found themselves on the same ground now as the woman caught in adultery. Their sin and her sin fell into the same classification of all sin! Each one had to deal with his own inner darkness.

Jesus was acting in faith as the light of the world. Light reveals what is in the darkness of our world - John 8:5-7, 12; Deuteronomy 17:7.

These lawyers, scribes, and Pharisees were now personally concerned. What was Jesus going to do? What seemed 'cut and dried' and proven was now in question. What exposing questions might Jesus ask of them next? They had no interest in seeking personal forgiveness for they were proud, arrogant men who now faced the possibility of losing face, power and relationship with their Roman invaders and financial resource.

They quickly and quietly started walking away as Jesus continued to write in the dust on the pavement. What he wrote is not known, but the results had them walking away one by one, from the oldest to the youngest. They vanished, probably hoping that no one in the crowd would ever recognize them again.

Jesus and the woman were finally alone.

Jesus, who had been kneeling in the dust writing, stood up and saw no one else other than the woman. It was the sinless Jesus who now had the right to throw the first stone.

As Augustine wrote, "At this time two persons were left, the unhappy woman and compassion incarnate." Obviously, the crowd was still present, but Jesus focused on the one person with the need.

Jesus Christ asked her, "Who condemns you?" She answered, calling him Lord. She makes no excuses but comes right to the point. She does not blame her accusers but responds directly as a sinner. "No one accuses me, Lord," she said. Christ, the only sinless one replied, "I forgive you: go and sin no more!" In other words, "Stop it!" He is not condemning, nor judgmental, but opens the merciful door of God's wonderful grace.

The perfect, endless, favor of God with an immediate acquittal, no more guilt. This door once opened encourages hope for the future and guilt is not the last word!

The law which calls for just judgment is under the gospel of Jesus Christ made to withdraw its demands. It is silenced forever by the compassionate love of Christ available through his death for all sin on our behalf!

Jesus Christ showed that faith abounds in an environment of forgiveness, mercy, and compassionate love. Guilt built upon activities and decisions made earlier in our life can misshape and even paralyze today's personal faith expression in God's promises.

For every believer, the old is passed away, all things are new, sin no longer has dominion over us, and the blood of Jesus has washed us clean. God has dissolved all faith-destroying guilt.

Embrace this truth, believe it and release your powerful, guilt free, personal faith - 2 Corinthians 5:17; Romans 6:14; Revelation 1:6.

Invest at all times in the nature of Christ – it is yours! Remind yourself from time to time that the Bible says, "Clothe yourself in him."

Take the higher ground whenever you are caring for people and exercise faith for that moment in your daily living.

You will always be a blessing to others, and what you have faith for in your life is bound to happen.

The promises of God are on display through our words and our actions. Faith achievements from this kind of openness of heart and generosity of spirit are guaranteed!

THE REVIEW

Step #5 Turn up the light.

Light reveals what is in the darkness of our world. Jesus taught sin is any action which contravenes Bible truth. What is Jesus to say to these men who caught this woman in the act of adultery? Each one had to deal with his own inner darkness. Jesus, the Light had exposed the hidden.

Reflections and personal observations -

My immediate thoughts

My life application

My personal example

My experience

My lessons learned

STEP #6

Faith Comes Out of the Closet

Some great achievers know what it is like to be 'written off' by critics as failures.

They succeeded! Regardless of these setbacks! These 'greats' are great because they weathered the storm of opposition, deserved or otherwise and became prominent leaders. They had a belief in their ability, rather like we have a belief that a particular chair will hold our weight.

Such a self-confidence and God-given faith are easily thought to be the same. But, there is a major difference between the two. Faith in God and faith that comes from life experience and natural confidence have very different foundations.

One is entirely dependent on God; the other is not! That's the difference.

Several important world leaders have had this type of career reversal.

They are found in industry, politics, scientific research, education and many other fields of endeavor.

It's rather like those things we resurrect around the home. A piece of clothing we own suddenly gains our attention again; that photograph, hobby, relationship and friendship, that holiday idea, part of my life which I have sadly neglected...

Suddenly that something or someone becomes accessible and useful again.

In the case of a person, the scrap heap of life transition begins with a rebirth. The 'new look' makes them valuable once again. That individual comes under the spotlight of a nation, industry or community group. Acknowledged as having an invaluable understanding of a particular crisis or circumstance, that 'someone' is popular again.

There was no more remarkable career reversal than that of Winston Churchill.

Minister for the Navy in the British government during World War I, Churchill was held responsible for the disastrous Dardanelles campaign. The voice of his critics dominated the news media of the day. His political party sacrificed him.

He was the scapegoat, the man who bore the anger of Parliament and rapidly became yesterday's man among the thinking public of Great Britain.

In World War II to whom did the British public turn? They turned to the once discredited Winston Churchill for leadership.

'Transformation' aptly describes his career reversal. Affectionately called Winnie he became wartime leader of the free world! The public respected him again.

Recall the story of Moses. For 40years a Prince in Egypt, adopted by the Monarchy and groomed for the highest office. Then an abrupt career reversal! Accused with real evidence of supporting a despised minority tribe and murder, Moses fled Egypt. He became a fugitive in the desert herding sheep.

God then chose him to lead his people like he chose the imprisoned, later Prime Minister Joseph; the ostracized desert runaway, later King David.

Both fear and faith compete for the believer's attention to the circumstances like this.

Fear says, "You have absolutely no possibility of success."

Faith says, "With the wisdom gathered from the past, and God's mentoring this is your opportunity."

Jesus Christ knew he was a rejected leader early in his life. But the characteristic of leaders who are first rejected and then recycled in this world is that they never give up. They know their destiny.

John, the disciple who had close associations with Jesus, declared he came to his own, and his own did not receive him. In fact, they rejected Christ outright – John 1:1-12.

Nevertheless, Jesus never gave up. As Peter, the leader of the early church described it, Jesus went about doing good, healing and comforting all who were oppressed by the enemy.

Evidence of his rejection was conspicuous in a continually growing opposition by the leadership of the Jewish people. Jesus was well aware of what this meant. He mentioned directly to his disciples on three different occasions his death – Acts 10:38.

Jesus never lets this opposition influence his faith and confidence. He maintained a clear, healthy relationship with his Father, God, which he upheld by prayer and every expectation of faith.

He said, "I only do what my Father does" and it took a Roman soldier with a sick servant to recognize this truth.

Coming to Jesus Christ in faith, with high expectation for his seriously sick servant the soldier declared, "Like you, Jesus, I am a man under authority." The Roman Commander then went on to say, "I am not spiritually qualified enough to have you enter my house so only speak out the word and my servant will be healed" - Matthew 8:5-10.

Jesus declared that this man's belief was an amazing example of faith. He then proceeded to reward his faith with the comment, "As you have believed, it has happened." The soldier returned home and found his servant healed.

The faith of this commander was founded on what he knew and saw in Jesus.

He publicly acknowledged the apparent relationship of Jesus Christ with his Father God. The soldier indicated, this to be the foundation for his faith in Christ. It must also be our foundation for personal faith in the living God - John 5:19-30.

The world and people pass judgment not only on the Winston Churchill's of life but also on you and me.

You may have had critics in your life who put you down with negative, depressing language. Your parents might have said to you, probably in the heat of the moment, "You will never amount to anything."

Perhaps others have said, "Who do you think you are?" A schoolteacher may have indicated that you have no future and put you in the lowest ten percent of the class.

When you were young, there may have been adults who betrayed your trust, even used and abused you as a teenager, making you feel worthless.

The stories are endless, and we can all add our own.

These words can rule and also ruin our life. Surprisingly some people never fear such occurrences. They just turn the negatives into positives and begin to shine again.

Winston Churchill is a case in point.

Another is the great classical composer Ludwig Van Beethoven who tragically lost his hearing but went on to compose his immortal Choral Symphony after he was deaf. Retired and on welfare, 'Colonel' Sanders began the Kentucky Fried Chicken chain.

Raised in severe poverty was Abraham Lincoln who became President of USA. A slow learner said to have no future was Albert Einstein, the acknowledged genius.

Rev. John Bunyan experienced time in prison where he wrote his epic, "Pilgrim's Progress."
British Prime Minister Benjamin Disraeli suffered severe religious prejudice, and the great hymn composer Fanny Crosby was born blind.

None of these historically famous people feared the shadows of their birth or their deficiencies and disabilities or what people thought of them.

By taking a faith action, we need to turn the negatives into positives. It was Jesus who said, "He who hears what I am saying and believes in my Father God who sent me will have a new kind of life."

Our choices define our faith.

A unique breakthrough comes in accepting those words of Jesus. A change so startlingly different it will be like passing from 'death to life!'

We can always continue to live in the shadows with life's uncertainties, or like the Roman Commander recognize the authority source of Jesus and enjoy God's favor.

Believe the words of Christ, the Son of God and "As you have believed let it done for you."

Break the power of those negative experiences and critical comments by believing that Bible truth. Faith always embraces God's word.

Prayer contacts God while faith obtains an audience.

Prayer quotes the promise while faith claims it.

Prayer is conscious of the need while faith supplies it.

Early computers would sometimes run very slow, becoming very sluggish in their operations. They would have to be 'defragged.'

This general process of tidying up the files restores the speed of the computer.

Sometimes we need to be subject to a defrag! We need to defrag the files of our mind especially. Unfinished business, loose ends, half starts, failed ideas, broken relationships.

When the Bible say's we are wrong, we should admit it. Jesus is only too happy to forgive us and to defrag us of all that is not right and is out of God's order.

Clear the way for real faith to start working within our life, producing a faith expression that will speed up our hearing, seeing and embracing of God's intended best for us. Useful files! Completed files! God purposed thinking! - Romans 8:1; 1 John 1:9.

The Jewish leadership had judged and condemned a woman as an adulteress. The penalty was death by stoning. Jesus raised himself from the ground where he'd been writing and saw no one else, but the woman – all of her accusers had gone.

Jesus speaks, and he does not minimize or cover up her sin but says, "Stop it!" He's not condemning in his comment - John 8:10-11.

The result was that the woman left Christ with hope but not guilt in this last word he spoke.

Guilt cripples personal faith. That's the reason Jesus gave the woman hope and freedom. We may not fully understand this level of forgiveness nor its releasing power from guilt.

Believe it, and walk in that new-found freedom. Jesus on another occasion said, "He who the Son sets free is indeed totally free" - John 8:32, 36. Blemished faith is weak faith. We have a choice.

We can believe our mind and the accusations of others. We can also choose to live in our self-imposed condemnation and guilt. With this choice, you will be heading for disappointment and an inferior life.

Jesus stated, "For as the Father has a life to give so he has granted me, the Son, to have life in myself and he has given me authority which includes judging also."

We must never ignore this truth, no matter how we feel personally, even if feeling unworthy of forgiveness.

Jesus swept away the self-judgement by saying, "You will know the truth, and the truth shall set you free of this dangerous thinking."

We must avoid a mindset which fails to grasp and accept the full extent of the forgiveness available through Jesus Christ. It is a choice only we can make - John 5:26-28.

Jesus reinforces this thinking in his story of a wise man building on the rock and a foolish man building on the sand. "He who hears my words and does them is like a wise man who, when the storms come because his house is built on the rock it will not topple, or be damaged in any way by the storm" – Matthew 7:24-25

It could be that 'our' faith has been found to be ineffective in a recent storm. That failure may sponsor a thinking pattern which says, "I'm not good enough."

Here we have the foundations for a great comeback and a great career-reversal assuring a true God-given resurrection. "He who hears my words and does them," Jesus said. Let's not explain the Bible away or justify our failures. Believe the quality and power of forgiveness God can release into our life. Believe...

Remember the religious Peter saying, "I will lay down my life for your sake," and three denials later he claimed that he never knew Jesus. That's when the rooster crowed, and Peter ran away in the anguish of heart, aware of his lack of faith and commitment to Jesus Christ.

Now move to the next frame, and we see a new Peter, drenched in the Spirit of God, a spokesman for the emerging dynamic group of believers in the Bible Book of Acts!

Now that's a great comeback! We are glad to know that God is incurably forgiving! He creates 'come back' moments for all who repent and call on him for help. With all our new beginnings we should hear his words and do exactly as directed.

Like the woman caught in adultery; like Peter, the liar we can know freedom from guilt by listening and acting on the words of Jesus Christ.

Faith is the world of power beyond the wilderness of human limitations.

Shake off every thought opposed to the fact that Jesus Christ has made us free. He has liberated us from guilt, condemnation and all the inroads of disappointments and failures in our life.

Always realize faith is the essence or substance of all those things that you want.

Our health, the supply of every need, positive relationships and more than enough life and faith to follow Jesus – Romans 8:1.

THE REVIEW

Step #6 Prayer quotes the promise while faith claims it!

Jesus knew he was a rejected leader early in life, but he continued doing good. You may have had these words spoken to you over your life - "You will never amount to anything." or, "Who do you think you are?" These words can rule, even ruin our life. Our choices define our faith.

Reflections and personal observations -

My immediate thoughts

My life application

My personal example

My experience

My lessons learned

STEP #7

Faith Is A Language

A sporting commentator attributed the extraordinary success of a particular football team to the ability of its players to talk to each other while they played. What they said to their teammates and the manner in which they spoke was also seen as important. The actual words spoken created a positive or negative atmosphere.

Sport is not the only realm where talk is important. For much the same reason Christians need to learn to speak in a faith encouraging way.

The words and the manner of delivery create a positive mindsct, a challenge to attitudes and lead us out of our problems.

Words will move us out of our moment of uncertainty into solutions and release through our personal application of faith in God's promises – James 3:1 – 12; Matthew 12:34. Whenever we turn to our Bibles, we discover many wonderful promises.

They relate to God's power to heal our bodies and to deliver us from all of the life's hurts.

Our Bible tells us God is for us. His power is available for us to apply in our daily living. He wants us to have health and strength through faith in his word.

We can prosper in all our activities because that is God's intended plan for us!

God initiated this plan by allowing his Son, Jesus Christ to live and die on this earth. Like a soldier dying in battle and sacrificing his life for the freedom of others, so Jesus died in our place. As a soldier's sacrifice affords freedom to his fellow citizens, so Jesus Christ has released us from the tyranny of evil, with the sin and the sickness we see surrounding us in this world - John 8:32, 36.

God offered his own Son as a sacrifice, allowing him to protect us from the attacking force of evil. His death on our behalf was so successful we can now reunite with God by choice. We can exercise a believing faith which brings us by spiritual birth into the family of God.

When connected to Father God in this way, he wants to protect us, provide for us, and be the loving parent he has promised to be.

How much space in my life do I give God? As Proverbs states; 'Fools are headstrong and do what they like; wise people take advice.' Let's keep that connection to Father God secure - John 1:12; Romans 8:32.

But wrong belief as a believer can also take us into an unbelieving faith. It is here we ignore the historical action of Jesus and become infected by the battle zone of sickness and failure surrounding us in this world.

God did not reduce the pain and price of death. He loaded it all on his Son. Jesus took it all in his body.

The death penalty which Jesus paid for us freed us to walk away acquitted. He took my sin and carried the full penalty for it and did this for every person living on Planet Earth.

God gave Jesus the suffering we should have endured. My sin was heaped upon Christ when he died in my place. So was the sin of every man woman and child of every generation following the death of Jesus Christ, God's only Son.

Every blessing of God, everything we, the believer, needs comes through this generous gift from Jesus allowed by Father God. It is now available to us for free by what Jesus did for us.

And we receive it all by faith - Ephesians 1:3; 2:8-10; James 1:17. We always have a choice. It was Paul, the writer of the book of Romans, who declared, "What shall we say to these things?" - Romans 8:31.

Well, what do you say to these things? Do you say God is against you? Do you say that life is against you? Do you continually speak about all the things and people who are against you?

Or, do you believe God's Word? Do you declare that God is for you? Do you believe because God is for you no one can overcome and defeat you? That's believing-faith.

Notice Paul did not say, "What shall we believe about these things?" That is critical. What Paul said was, "What shall we say to these things?"

Let's come back to our sporting team that attributed its success to the way they talked to one another on the field. It is well near impossible for you to believe that God is for you if you continually speak of the things that are against you.

Don't dwell on the problems; rise above them when they are disrupting your life. Guard your faith against any possibility of storm damage by being careful as to what you say.

Conversation based upon doubt and uncertainty will always weaken our faith– Matthew 21:21. Solomon said that death and life are in the power of the tongue. He also said, "With the increase of his lips shall he be filled."

So we see the tremendous power of the words that we speak. Our language determines our future, and if it's full of faith, then faith will be in our future, and the objects of faith will crowd out any negatives in our life.

What shall we say about these things? If God is for us, who can be against us?

Our words fill us the same way as the food we eat. More people are sick because of the words they have spoken than because of what they eat. Someone said stomach ulcers are not caused by what you eat but by what's eating you. And, friends, most people want to talk about what's eating them! Yes, there's an incredible power in the words we speak, and they can destroy Bible faith working in our lives – Jeremiah 15:16.

It is time we agreed that God is with us. It's not sensible to talk ourselves out of the blessings and miracles that God has promised us. People say, "I cannot deny my symptoms; I cannot deny the facts; I cannot deny the difficulties that I am facing in life."

It is not what we deny but what we affirm that counts. We cannot deny that things are against us, but we can state the things that are for us.

God's will and his Word are for us. Believe it, and declare it.

God is a good God. It is certain the devil is against us, sin is against us, sickness is against us, and maybe many people are against us. We cannot deny these things, but we can turn our back on them and affirm this glorious truth that God is for us! And if God is for us then we are compelled to ask who can be against us? That is, who can stop us or defeat us if God is for us?

Let's grow our faith by changing our language. Let our words mirror our thinking.

God is not the author of adverse happenings in your life. He is not against you; he is for you. It is his will to deliver you from the tormenting fears and complexities that come with the storms of life. But stand in faith releasing the Word of God into your circumstances.

The Bible says God will freely give you all things. No good thing will he withhold from those who walk in the truth and act on that Bible truth - Psalm 84:11.

The Bible also declares, "I wish above all things that you may prosper and be in health even as your soul – mind and emotions – prospers." See 3 John 2.

We can continue telling you how and why God is for you. But remember the greatest proof and demonstration of this fact is what God allowed Jesus to go through for us on the cross where he died.

It was there Christ paid the price for our peace, joy and good health in this life. So, have a generous faith for personal miracles! Believe God's promise!

Live with a 'God can' attitude and speak words which reflect this confidence in Him!

Take this step of faith. Disregard all opposition and distractions that attempt to derail your faith action. Deny all thinking which would put you off course and dilute your expectations.

Like Peter declared, *"Nevertheless, at your word I will let down the net (of faith)."* Hold firmly to that confession of faith without any uncertainty or wavering for God is faithful who promised to do it – Hebrews 10:23.

THE REVIEW

Step #7 It is not what we deny but
what we affirm that counts.

It is almost impossible for you to believe that God is for
you if you continually speak of what is against you. Don't
dwell on the problems. Conversation based upon doubt
and uncertainty will always weaken personal faith.

Reflections and personal observations -

My immediate thoughts

My life application

My personal example

My experience

My lessons learned

AUTHOR PROFILE:

Born and educated in Perth, Western Australia, David Rodway graduated with honors from the University of Western Australia. Later he completed a Masters degree, while employed in the Office of the Premier of South Australia. At the same time, he also completed Bible College and a Ministry Development Course.

David and Cherie met in Adelaide, South Australia and married in 1970. They led Adelaide's then fastest growing youth group with hundreds finding faith in Jesus Christ.

In 1973, they joined the ministry team led by Pastor Leo Harris, founder of the Christian Revival Crusade and served in various capacities until the early 1990's.

During this time, David also lectured and tutored at the University of South Australia, and taught in Bible Colleges and designed curriculums for Bible Courses.

A passion for teaching and explaining Bible truths began to emerge. His heart was for people to know Jesus and make Him known; and, to build faith people.

Supporting families in this vision made him a driving force behind the beginnings of Sunrise Christian schools in the 1970's and the founding Chairman of the secondary school, Temple Christian College.

His belief in the Bible as the textbook for everyday life made his practical messages on faith sought after.

Today more than 8,000 people follow him on various social media platforms worldwide. David is comfortable and experienced in speaking to a few or, to hundreds.

This passion for teaching a life based active personal faith in God's Word brought David and Cherie to Canada in 2007.

They have been teaching, and writing books, including a book series for children and ministering at 'The Ledge,' Canada, with an emphasis on growing faith-filled people and providing an opportunity to revive, renew and recover from the wounds of life.

Made in the USA
San Bernardino, CA
05 November 2018